1

THE CORNISH FAMILY:

A Reference Work for Genealogists

THE AMERICAN SURNAME SERIES

Ryan P. Jordan, Ph.D

Editor

Preface

The study of family history, or genealogy, is one of the oldest human pursuits. Genealogies of Egyptian Pharaohs date back more than 3,000 years; the descendants of Adam were written about more than 2,500 years ago in the Book of Genesis; and in China, dynastic records of aristocratic families are often more than 2,000 years old. Roman genealogies as well as the genealogy of Jesus Christ date from the first century in the Common Era. Many of the current royal families of Europe can accurately trace their ancestry back to the sixth century, or more than 1,400 years ago.

Practically every great civilization in history has found organization in the family— whether it is the small nuclear family of the present, or the larger multigenerational clans of earlier times. The pedigrees and lines of succession used by royal families today are just one way that people keep track of their personal, local, ethnic or national story. It is almost natural that people have some kind of curiosity regarding their origins, and when people undertake the pursuit of genealogy, they soon find how interrelated they are to the larger nations and ethnic groups from which they descend. No one should take too much pride in the uniqueness of their ancestry at some point, since nearly everyone has royals and commoners, famous and obscure ancestors and relatives in their family tree—it is just a question of whether you can prove the connection.

This book is a small, but important record of the **Cornish** family, in an effort to aid beginning genealogists in their hunt for ancestors. From the feudal period to seventeenth century Britain and the settling of North America, to the Revolution and Civil War, members of the **Cornish** family have played a part in the history of Western Europe and the United States.

In the following pages, you will find information on the origin of the family name, the armorial heritage, and the biographies of the more famous bearers of this surname. Likely a relative or cousin of yours is mentioned here, and hopefully the story told will inspire you to seek out more details regarding your own family's heritage.

The Surname Cornish

The surname **Cornish** is a name of English, French, and Cornish origin seen throughout the British Isles and the United States. The name can also be found in Australia, New Zealand, and parts of Africa. The name **Cornish** is used by many African-Americans in the United States, as well.

According to data derived from the 2010 US Census, the surname **Cornish** is ranked 2,783 in the United States, with approximately 12,000 people using this last name. The variants of **Cornish** are Cornwall, Cornwallis, Cornell, Cornhill, Corneille, among others.

The name **Cornish**, and its variants, comes from one of five origins:

1) Someone from a place named Cornwell, an example being Cornwell, Oxfordshire, England

2) Someone from the province of Cornwall, in England—or someone identified as Cornish, or "Cornwalish"

3) Someone from places named Cornhill, of which there used to be one in London,

England, or for some other association with corn.

4) Possibly originating with the French, Corneille, a "rook or a crow", meaning someone who was a chatterer, or who came from an area where crows lived

What's In a Name?

Building a genealogy or family tree obviously begins with a surname. But do you know where your last name came from? For those trying to trace their family back many centuries, do you know how your name was spelled two, three, or five centuries ago? While it may not be possible to know precisely why you have your last name, understanding the various ways your ancestors may have spelled their surname could go a long way to helping you trace your family tree back generations—and it may even provide surprising information regarding your family's ethnic background.

Surnames arose for several reasons in Europe—and became fixed, or hereditary—at different times. Students of surnames explain that there were four general ways that a surname came into existence:

1) Surnames derived from a parent's first name—called "patronymics." Examples include Johnson, Richardson, or Carlson.

2) Surnames derived from a location, or place where one worked or owned land—called "toponymics." Examples include Brooke, Rivers, or England.

3) Surnames derived from one's type of work—otherwise known as occupational surnames. Examples include Smith, Miller, or Fisher.

4) Surnames derived from a nickname, or some other personal attribute (such as ethnicity, appearance, or character)—these are also sometimes called "ornamental" surnames. Examples include Short, Greathead, Good, or Gold.

But, as will be discussed below, a surname often had multiple origins, since it can be difficult to figure why any one particular family assumed a name spelled or pronounced a certain way. This is where genealogy comes in.

In some countries surnames became hereditary more recently than others. Many parts of England, Scotland, France, Spain, Switzerland, and Italy, had hereditary surnames at least by 1550 (with some families claiming the same name as far back as the 1000s A.D.). Meanwhile other countries in Europe—most notably Holland, Sweden,

Norway, Denmark, Iceland, as well as Muslim parts of Europe, such as Bosnia—did not develop surnames until the 1700s, or even later. Those of Jewish descent in all European countries also often only took names in the 1700 or 1800s.

In the case of Scandinavia, most rural people were not required to take hereditary surnames until the mid and late 1800s. So for example, in the case of Denmark, many of the Jensens and Nielsens alive today are only five or at most six generations removed from the original Jens or Niels who gave them their names. Before the early 1800s, sons and daughters simply used the name of their father for one generation as a second name (Niels Larson meant Niels son of Lars). Many families in other Northern European countries know exactly when and how they acquired their last name, because it occurred within the time frame of modern church records that have been preserved. In the case of the Slecht or Slaight of New York, the family can be traced to court records in the town of Woerden, Holland. There is preserved an interesting record of a man named Gerrit Jan Peiter Floriszoon who, in June 1609 earned the name "Slechten" or "Slecht"--meaning bad-- for his violent protests against taxes owed to the local sheriff. From the early 1600s forward, Gerrit's children and grandchildren would take the last name Slecht from their ancestor's run in with the law.

Still, even when surnames became hereditary, this did not stop succeeding generations from modifying the spelling of their name.

To take the example of the surname Jerdan, just in the last 250 years, the name has been spelled many ways, ranging from Jourdaine, Jerdon, Jordon, Gardine and Gardyne. The variety of spelling points to the multiple possible origins of the surname as well since both Jerdan and Gardine are actually variants of the Anglo-Norman Jardin (meaning "one from a garden" or "gardener") while the other spellings stem from the Anglo-Norman Jourdan, meaning "one from a place called Jordan" (modern spelling), or "the son of Jordan."

It is important to remember that before the modern era of driver's licenses, Social Security cards, passports, IRS tax ID numbers and other state-issued ID, people had fewer interactions with the state—or were less thoroughly identified by the government-- and therefore had fewer reasons to care about the exact spelling of their surname. Also note that in earlier eras literacy rates were far lower than today, and many others were only partially literate—so keeping track of an exact spelling of a surname may have been harder to do.

There are other factors to keep in mind when understanding possible, earlier versions of your surname. An important one has to do with the changing linguistic boundaries in Europe. For example, in the case of the old Austrian or Austro-Hungarian Empire many people spoke more than one language, and depending on various local political or economic reasons the numbers and relative power of one linguistic group would change over time in the same locale. This often meant that later generations spoke a different language than earlier ones.

In many parts of modern-day Slovakia for example, peasants that earlier in the nineteenth century spoke primarily Slovakian or German later came under more direct rule of Hungarians and felt pressure for various reasons to change their name. So people with the surname Zajacz (which means rabbit in Slovakian) took on the Hungarian version of the name, Nyulaszi when under pressure from new rulers. Germans in the area who had been named Mueller (meaning Miller) might later take on the Hungarian name Molnar that had the same meaning. Understanding the ethno-linguistic changes and political background of the regions where your ancestors came from can be crucial in establishing links to earlier versions of your surnames in the same place but with a different language.

Likewise, migration within different regions of Europe—or even between different states or principalities within the same country—often meant that surnames changed, or at least their spelling did. In what is today northeastern Italy, the Friulian language (of the Romansch family) was widely spoken, alongside Italian. But either by moving to other parts of the same province where more Italian was spoken, or by moving to a different region of the Italian peninsula, a person's surnames could change and change drastically.

For example, the surname Varnaran, which belongs to the Friulian dialect of Italian and means someone who was a soldier, or who guarded things, often became Guarnerini when its holders moved among standard Italian speakers. Another example of a surname change within Italy based on regional variations is the surname Santin, which is Venetian, but becomes Santini or Santino in other parts of Italy.

Elsewhere in Europe, French Protestant (Huguenot) refugees often adapted their names to their surroundings when they moved to England. The French surname Doucet could become Dawcett after a few years in Great Britain. In Spanish speaking countries, many

Basque names likewise became modified by their bearers after years of living among Spaniards—such as the Basque name Baztan becoming Bazan in Spanish.

Upon immigration to the United States, many surnames became Anglicized—and this trend did not just begin with larger non-English emigration in the late 1800s. Many German, Dutch, and French immigrants in the 1600s adapted their names to the English language. Examples include the German Schmidt becoming Smith; the French D'Auge becoming Dage; and the Dutch surname van Nieuwkerk simply becoming Newkirk after a few generations in New York.

In the period after 1880, many Polish, Russian, and Italian emigrants changed their names to fit in, to more easily get jobs, or because of aggressive efforts at Americanization. This could be especially true of Jewish immigrants and their children. Entertainer Jack Benny was actually born Benjamin Kubelsky and comedian George Burns was born Nathan Birnbaum. But immigrants from countries that had been sending people across the Atlantic for centuries also changed their surnames, like the English born Arthur Stanley Jefferson, who arrived in the United States in the 1910s, and became Stan Laurel, rising to fame as one part of the Laurel and Hardy act.

All of these kinds of changes and others can impact your search into your family's origins, and you should keep an open mind regarding the many earlier spellings of your last name.

In the case of the surname **Cornish** there are several other spellings that have been associated with this name for more than five hundred years. Below are just some of the spelling variants that have been associated with the last name:

Cornewelle, Cornwall, Cornewale, Cornwaleys Cornwallis, Cornes Cornell, Corneille, Cornhill, Cornhell, Cornhill, Cornmell

Earliest Origins

In England, early references to the surname **Cornish** and its variants can be found from the 1100s and include:

Roger de Cornwelle, living in 1161 in Oxfordshire, England

Geruase de Cornhill, living in 1179 in Kent

William Corneille, living in 1206 in London

Henry de Cornell, living in 1230 in London

Henry le Cornwaleys, living in 1256 in Hampshire

William Cornysh, born 1430, living in London

Edmund Cornewall, born in 1488 in Shropshire, England

Robert Cornwell, of Biddenden, Kent, England, adult in 1563

Thomas Cornwell, of Norfolk, England, in 1573

Gabriel Cornwell, of Herefordshire, England, adult in 1574

Thomas Cornwell, of St. Mary Cray, Kent, England, adult in 1592

Christopher Cornwell, adult of Lincoln, England in 1611

In Wales, the surname is found as early as the late 1500s:

Elena Cornhill, born to parents of the name in Montgomeryshire in 1617

John Corwall, born to parents named Corwall in 1620 in Montgomeryshire, Wales

Richard Cornish, died in 1687, in Cardiff, Wales

William Cornish, alive in 1689, in Cardiff, Wales

William Cornewell, in Bridgend, Glamorganshire, Wales in the late 18th and early 19th century

In Ireland, the surname is found as early as the 1600s:

James Cornish, adult in 1695 in Dublin, Ireland

John Cornwell, adult in 1697 in Dublin, Ireland

William Cornish, adult in 1697 in Dublin, Ireland

Benjamin Cornwell, adult in 1698, in Dublin, Ireland

William Cornwell, adult in the late 18th century in Down, Ireland

In Scotland, the name and its variants are seen in the late 1500s:

Andrew Cornell, lived in 1594 in Fife, Scotland

Peter Cornell, lived in 1595 in Edinburgh, Scotland

John Cornwell, in Inveresk, Midloathian, Scotland, living in 1629

James Cornwell, in Fife, Scotland, living in 1648

George Cornwell, of Edinburgh, living in 1633

John Cornwell, East Lothian, Scotland, living in 1634

Further Reading

Basil Cottle, *The Penguin Dictionary of Surnames* (Penguin,1986)

J.N Hook, *Family Names: The Origins, Meanings, Mutations, and History of More Than 2,800 American Names* (Collier, 1982)

P.H. Reany, *A Dictionary of English Surnames: The Standard Guide to English Surnames* (Oxford, 1995)

Elsdon C. Smith, *American Surnames* (Chilton Books, 1969)

The

Cornish Surname and the Nobility

Many early examples and variants of the surname **Cornish** were reserved for varying branches of the nobility and royalty. In the societies that existed in the period when surnames came into existence (1000AD to 1500 AD) often—though not always—the most powerful and wealthy social class were those who in some way owned a "fief"—meaning the right to own land, or collect rents and taxes from land owned by an overlord such as a Duke or King. In return for the right to owner the fief holder pledged allegiance to his overlord often in the form of financial and military service to the noble who gave him the fief, and the owner of the fief was responsible for the peasants and serfs (unfree laborers) who lived on the property.

Among the overlords in this system of feudal nobility can be found several hereditary titles that referred to men of higher nobility.

In most parts of Europe, the ranking of nobles was usually as follows:

King / Emperor / Grand Duke/ Archduke: these were sovereign heads of state

Prince: A member of the royal family, or another royal who does not exercise power as head of state

Duke / Sovereign Prince/ Fuerst: Owner of very large duchy estates, and often related to a prince or king, but generally not the ruler of a state

Marquis / Landgrave / Margrave: Customarily ranked higher than a count because of larger military responsibility and political power within the realm.

Count / Earl: A title often used for those in direct service to royalty, or for a member of a minor branch of a royal family.

Viscount/ Vidame: Traditionally someone in service to a count, and the title was not always hereditary.

Baron: Those who hold land directly from the King, or those who owed political responsibility directly to a king or sovereign, but who themselves possessed less land and political power than Counts and Viscounts.

Baronet/ Hereditary Knight: A more privileged, wealthier knight whose title is hereditary

Since the first recording of the name **Cornish** and its variants there have been members of the upper nobility with the surname. Examples include:

Charles Cornwallis, First Marquis Cornwallis (1738-1805)

Fiennes Stanley Wyckeham Cornwalis, Baron Cornwalis (1864-1935)

As opposed to those possessing the above titles, the vast majority fief owners in the feudal system were gentlemen, esquires (squires), and knights. These titles refer to the lower nobility. Men in this category generally possessed smaller fiefs and in some cases their titles could not be inherited by their sons (though this varied depending on location and time period.) In the cases of esquires and knights, their positions were more formally tied to military service and they perhaps had more prestige and land than a simple gentlemen.

There have been numerous lower nobles with the surname **Cornish**. Examples include:

Sir John Cornewaille, English knight alive in the 1300s

Sir Thomas Cornwall, 1474-1537, English politician from Shropshire, England

Sir George Cornewalle, 1748-1819, of Moccas Court, Herefordshire, England

It has been estimated that at any given time in many European countries between 5-10% of the society belonged in some way to the nobility—but the vast majority were gentlemen, squires, or knights. All of these nobles also possessed the right to a coat of arms that could be passed along to the eldest son of the family.

Heraldry, or the study of coats of arms, is related to the study of family history. Coat armor became common in England and other parts of the British Isles after roughly 1250, even as its origins can be traced back to some of the Crusades, which began as early as 1097. The development of heraldic devices followed the development of surnames as a means of better identifying families for legal purposes. The use of coats of arms was also important as a means of identification in battle, but the art form of heraldry catered to the needs of nobles and aristocrats who sought to distinguish themselves from commoners. Later, merchants and professionals began designing arms for their families as well.

By the late 1500s, central authorities were established to inquire into the validity of the various coats of arms being minted, and heralds, as they were known, began investigating the genealogies of the families claiming certain designs. The thorough records of many of these heralds have been extremely useful for genealogists, and some of these records are included in the "further reading" section.

In the United States, since there is no formal aristocracy there are few coats of arms, though it is important to note that many corporations, government agencies, and political bodies have their own varieties of insignia that owe at least some inspiration to medieval heraldry.

Many surnames, such as **Cornish** have multiple coats of arms that have been used either officially or unofficially over the centuries. The following descriptions come from *Burke's Peerage* and are likely just a few of the coats of arms used by members of the **Cornish** family:

1) A red lion on a white shield (Cornwell)

2) Three black birds on a white crest (Cornwallis)

3) A black crest with three white flowers around a garter (Cornwall, Cornish)

Whether or not your direct male **Cornish** ancestor can be traced to the nobility it is likely that you have noble ancestry in some direction in your family tree, since if you could trace all of your ancestors back to the year 1200, you would likely have the same number of ancestors as the entire population of England at the time. (Of course, many of these are the same people, given the realities of intermarriage.) Going back just a few generations further and you have more ancestors than the population of Europe at the time.

Further Reading

Sir Bernard Burke, *The General Armory of England, Scotland, Ireland, and Wales* (London, 1884)

Frederick Crisp and Joseph Jackson Howard, *Visitation of England and Wales* 12 volumes, (London, 1893-1917)

Burke's Genealogical and Heraldic History of the Landed Gentry Including American Families with British Ancestry (London, 1939)

William Armstrong Crozier, *Crozier's General Armory, a Register of American Families Entitled to Coat Armor* (Baltimore, 1966)

W.H Whitmore, *The Heraldic Journal: Recording the Armorial Bearings and Genealogies of American Families* (Baltimore, 1972)

See also:
http://www.heraldryonline.org.uk/Archivebook
slinks.htm

Early Townsmen and Merchants Named Cornish

In many towns and cities of late medieval and early modern Europe (roughly 1200-1600) various merchants, doctors or lawyers who were not directly part of the feudal hierarchy (meaning that they did not derive income from properties given by overlords or royalty), but these men nonetheless acquired wealth and social standing similar to that of the lower nobility. In many cases these families were also entitled to use a coat of arms. Additionally, the daughters of wealthy merchants or professionals might be able to marry into the nobility, especially since some noble families had fallen on hard times financially.

Some examples of early city dwellers in **London, Dublin** and elsewhere named **Cornish** (and variants) include:

Arthur Cornwall married to Fortune Petch, in 1603 in London

Nicholas Cornewall, born in 1574 in London

Clement Cornwell, of London alive in the 1500s

John Cornwell, who witnessed baptism of son Richard in 1570 in London

John Cornwell, who with wife Judith witnessed baptism of on Daniel, in 1581 in London

John Cornish, adult in 1586 in London

Thomas Cornwallis, adult in 1591 in London

Rislee Cornwallis, born in 1598 in London

William Cornwell, of London, alive in the early 1600s

Giels Cornish, adult in 1646 in London

John Cornish, adult in 1650 in London

Christopher Cornish, adult in 1662 in London

Thomas Cornwell, of London, alive in the mid 1600s

John Cornwell, alive in the 1600s in Dublin, Ireland

Peter Cornell, present for christening of daughter Rachel, in 1604, in Edinburgh, Scotland

George Cornwallis married to Dorothy Jegin, 1619, in London

James Cornell married to Janet Yodle, in 1629 in Edinburgh, Scotland

Henry Cornwell, who witnessed the baptism of a son, David in 1670 in Dublin, Ireland

Ebenezer Cornell, born in Dublin in 1675

Jeremiah Cornell, born in 1678 in Dublin

Caleb Cornell, born in 1683 in Dublin, Ireland

Joshua Cornell, born in 1686 to Thomas in Dublin, Ireland

Phillip Cornwell, of Swansea, Wales at the turn of the 19th century

Staggard or Slaggart Cornwall, of Cardiff, Wales in the 19th century

By 1550, with the growth of many European states, and in addition to the Protestant Reformation, where both Catholics and Protestants wanted to keep track of their congregants—historians see an increase in church records and other documents that kept track of the population of countries like England, Scotland, or Ireland. Increasing numbers of commoners and peasants—people with little money, land, or education are included in these national records. Often, many average people could not read or write, and so spelling for surnames may not have been fixed, as they would be in later centuries. The church records of Britain from the mid 1500s on record many families of the name **Cornish**, and included below is a representative sampling from around the British Isles:

The family of Francis and Thomas Cornwallis, of Shropshire, England, living in the 1600s

The family of John and Thomas Cornwall, of Lancashire, England, in the 1700s

Charles Cornwallis, of Middlesex, England, living in the 1600s and early 1700s

Henry and Thomas Cornell, of Cheshire, England living in the late 1600s

William Cornell, of Cheshire, England living in the early 1700s

Jarvis Cornwell of Lincolnshire, England in the early 1700s

William, James, George, Samuel, and Thomas Cornell, living in Suffolk, England in the late 1700s

Joshua Cornwell of Northumberland, England in the late 1700s

William Cornwell of York, England in the late 1700s

Charles Corneille, living in 1840 in Middlesex, England

James Corneille, of Scotland, living in 1860 in London, England

John and Alice Corneille, of Ireland, living in Ireland in 1870

Further Reading

J.A. Bettey, *Church and Parish: A Guide for Local Historians* (London, 1987)

David Hey, *The Oxford Guide to Family History* (New York, 1993)

Stuart Raymond, *Parish Registers: A History and Guide* (Lancashire, 2009)

W.B. Stephens, *Sources for English Local History* (London, 1981)

K.M. Thompson, *Short Guides to Records* (London, 1972-1997)

Colonial Cornish Immigrants

When talking about his ancestry, Will Rogers famously joked that his ancestors (Rogers was part Cherokee) were at the dock to meet the Mayflower. This was meant to chasten anyone who took too much pride in their colonial ancestry, and Rogers had an important point. It has been estimated that at least 100 million Americans descend from some of the earliest settlers at Jamestown, Virginia (1607), New Amsterdam, later New York (1620), Plymouth (1620), or Boston (1630).

The first immigrants to what became the United States were the English along with their African slaves, followed by a few Dutch and Swedes, then the Scottish (including Scots from Ulster in Ireland) and Welsh, and then Germans, Irish Catholics, and still later people from nearly every part of the globe.

The early English immigrants arrived in three geographic centers: the tidewater of Virginia and Maryland beginning in 1607; to Massachusetts beginning in 1620; as well as to the Caribbean islands of St. Kitts, Barbados, and Nevis, beginning in 1623.

The English settlers to Virginia, who founded the Jamestown Colony in 1607, were attracted by the allure of easy riches that the Spaniards had found in central America. These early settlers were disproportionately from the gentry class and were therefore unprepared for the first winter in the New World. Many died in the so-called "Starving Time." However, reinforcements continued to arrive and with the discovery that tobacco grew well in the swampy soil, the fortunes of Virginia as well as Maryland, took a turn for the better. Over the course of many decades, indentured white servants (young people who signed contracts for generally five years) and later African slaves arrived in this colony along with the so-called "Cavaliers"—or wealthy sons of the lower nobility and gentry in England. Larger and larger plantations soon dotted the landscape of the southeast and a planter culture was born that sought to emulate the lives of the landed class in England. Many of the most prominent names in Revolutionary America—Washington, Jefferson, Madison, Monroe, Lee, and Randolph—descended from early Virginia planters, and many had family ties to the nobility in England.

Several members of the **Cornish** family arrived in the earliest decades of the Virginia colony and the South, seeking to establish farms or plantations of their own in the New World. Included among them were the following:

Edward Cornwall, living in 1697, in Richmond, Virginia

John and Martha Cornish, adults in 1678, living in Charles County, Maryland

Nicholas Cornewell, living in Somerset County, Maryland in 1690

John Cornwell b. 1743 d. 1778 of Prince William County, Virginia

Simon Cornwell, born in the 1740s in Virginia

John Cornish of Northumberland, Virginia, alive in 1739

John Cornell, born in 1750 in Stafford County, Virginia

Edward Cornwell of Cleveland County, North Carolina in the late 1700s

Thomas Cornwall, of Baltimore, Maryland, adult in 1790

William Cornwell, married to Mary Brown, 1789 in Surry, Virginia

Francis Cornwell, Pittsylvania County, Virginia, alive in the late 1700s

The second group of English colonists include the Puritans, a determined group of religious exiles who sought to create in North America what they could not have in England: a society ruled by and for the "godly." Puritans rejected what they saw as the laxity and corruption of both the Roman Catholic Church, as well as the Church of England in the seventeenth century. Puritans wanted to return to the simplicity of the Bible and what they would have called "the priesthood of all believers." They sought an exclusive fellowship of only those who had truly been "born again." Their righteous vision for society was obviously not all positive, as can be seen in the infamous Salem Witch Trials at the end of the 1600s. But the Puritans emphasis on education (they founded Harvard in 1630), as well as representative democracy embodied in town halls left a lasting impact on American culture.

The first group of Puritans (actually termed separatists as they sought to leave the Church of England and not simply reform it) arrived at Plymouth in 1620. Like the Jamestown settlers, they also endured much hardship, but thanks to the hospitality of local natives, the English survived. They also were said to have celebrated the first of many Thanksgiving days in American history.

Roughly ten years after the first settlers arrived at Plymouth, other Puritans, led by John Winthrop founded the city of Boston in 1630. Like many other Puritans, Winthrop actually came from the gentry class and was a well educated minister. Historians have noted the prominent social backgrounds of many Puritans, explaining that these immigrants did not come to the New World for economic reasons, but rather for religious and ideological ones: the Puritans were so convinced of the righteousness of their ways that they led an effort to first depose and later execute King Charles I, in the 1640s, an event that led to a civil war in England. But many of these Puritans, as genealogist Gary Boyd Roberts pointed out, were actually related to British royalty as descendants of younger sons of the nobility.

Among the many early New England immigrants included those with the name **Cornish** and its variants:

Thomas Cornell, Sr., emigrated before 1638 to Boston, ancestor of many prominent New Englanders

Thomas Cornell d. 1656 in Newport, Rhode Island

41

William Cornwell of Middlesex Connecticut emigrated before 1641

John Cornwell of Middlesex, Connecticut, before 1666

John Cornish, of Boston, 1686

Gabriel Cornish, 1691, Hampden, Massachusetts

Samuel Cornish, adult in 1694, in Plymouth, Massachusetts

John Cornwell married in 1695 to Elizabeth Hinsdall in Franklin, Massachusetts

George Cornell, Quaker, living in 1697 in Newport, Rhode Island

Abraham Cornwell, married in Boston to Hannah Sherrar in 1719

Richard Cornell, of Bristol, Massachusetts, adult in 1733

Rebecca Corneille, living in 1750 in New Hampshire

Joshua and Lewis Cornwall, of New York, before 1800

The third group of early English settlers included those who took their chances in the Caribbean. For many years after the successful colonization of Cuba, Mexico, and Peru by the Spanish, the English sought to get their share of the great fortunes in silver and other goods found in Central and South America. The infamous English "sea dogs" or pirates of the Caribbean—men like Francis Drake, John Hawkins, and Walter Raleigh—had long tried to move in on Spanish territory in the New World starting in the late 1500s. But permanent settlement of the English in Central America and the Caribbean did not start until the 1620s, when other English maritime adventurers, such as Sir Thomas Warner in St. Kitts (including Nevis) and John Powell in Barbados brought thousands of white indentured servants to the islands. Most of these men worked for absentee landlords, such as James, the Earl of Carlisle and Sir William Courten, but with time many white settlers acquired their own fortunes and established enormous sugar plantations in their own right by the 1660s.

By the late 17th century, Barbados and other English Caribbean colonies—most notably Jamaica—greatly expanded the English slave trade and increasingly used black labor instead of white servants to work the sugar plantations. By 1700, many Caribbean English families moved to the new colony of Carolina, based in Charleston, where they continued to own and develop plantations with black slaves. These Carolina families of Caribbean origin include the Drayton, Middleton, and the Yeamans of Yeamans Hall. Later in the 1700s, the Caribbean would send many families to the Northern Thirteen Colonies, including Alexander Hamilton (born in Nevis) who would later serve as the first Secretary of the Treasury.

Some of the early members of the **Cornish** family who emigrated to the Caribbean include:

William Cornwell, migrated to Barbados in 1635

Thomas Cornwell, alive in St. Catherine's, Jamaica in 1673

Thomas Cornish, born in 1760, in St. Elizabeth, Jamaica

Later migrants to colonies such as North and South Carolina, New York, Pennsylvania, include:

Benjamin Cornish, of 1716, in New York, New York

Henry Cornish, of Charleston, South Carolina, 1723

Joseph Cornwell, born in Philadelphia, in 1750

John Cornwall, who emigrated from Ireland to Philadelphia in the late 1700s

Gilliam Cornell, of Bucks, Pennsylvania, adult in 1770

Edward Cornwell of Cleveland County, North Carolina in the late 1700s

James Cornell, of Surry, North Carolina, adult in the 1790s

Further Reading

N. Dermott Harding, *Bristol and America, A Record of the First Settlers in the Colonies of North America, 1654-1685* (Baltimore, 1970)

John Camden Hotten, *Lists of Emigrants to America, 1600-1700* (Baltimore, 1968) and Hotten, *Original Lists of Persons of Quality...to the American Plantations, 1600-1700* (Baltimore, 1976)

Jack and Marion Kamnikow, *A List of Emigrants from England to America, 1718-1759* (Baltimore, 1964)

Frederick Virkus, *The Abridged Compendium of American Genealogy* (Baltimore, 1968)

Cornish Surname and the American Revolution

By the mid 1700s, the thirteen mainland colonies had grown remarkably in size. From a population under 300,000 in 1700, the success of the colonies had led the number of colonists to grow to 2 million by 1770. The cities of the eastern seaboard in many ways rivaled decent sized British towns and the complexity of the settlements required more and more oversight. For its part, Great Britain wanted more trade restrictions placed on the colonists (meaning that Britain did not want to compete with her colonial subjects on the foreign markets) and the mother country would eventually try to raise a revenue to pay for colonial administration, particularly after Britain's defeat of France in the Seven Years War nearly doubled the size of Britain's North American holdings.

The British colonists, on the other hand, increasingly saw themselves as having outgrown the British Empire. Tensions between the mother country and the colonists can be seen during the Seven Year's War itself, when colonial soldiers disliked taking orders from British officers. When asked to pay even more in taxes after 1765, the colonists made it clear the answer was no. The cry of "no taxation without representation" (meaning that the colonists could not sit in Parliament but could have taxes imposed on them by that institution) would eventually lead to rebellion in 1775 in Massachusetts, followed by further British military occupation of the colonies and independence being declared in 1776.

In the eighteenth century, many families with the surname **Cornish** lived throughout the thirteen colonies, and many served either in the colonial wars of the eighteenth century, held political office in the various colonies, or served in the Revolutionary War.

Here is a representative sample of **Cornish** and variant names during the Era of the American Revolution:

Ezekiel Cornell, Brigadier General, Rhode Island

Anthony Cornwall, Pennsylvania

Caleb Cornwall, New York

James Cornwall, New York

Richard Cornwall, Connecticut

Thomas Cornwall, Pennsylvania

Daniel Cornish, of Massachusetts

Elisha and George Cornish of Connecticut

John Cornish, of Delaware

John Cornish of Maryland

Joseph Cornell, Ensign, Rhode Island

Gabriel Cornish of Massachusetts

Ozious Cornwell, Massachusetts Militia

Richard Cornwell, New York Militia

William Cornwell, Hay's Regiment, Militia, New York

Joseph and Sylvennus Cornwell, New York Militia

Richard, Benjamin and Daniel Cornwell, Connecticut Sixth Regiment

Daniel Cornwell, Virginia Militia

Thomas and Daniel Cornwell, New York

Tyng Cornwell, Massachusetts

Samuel and Benjamin Cornell of New York

John Cornell of Delaware

Further Reading

Francis B. Heitman, *Historical Register of Officers of the Continental Army during the War of the Revolution, 1775-1783* (Baltimore, 1967)

Max Hoyt, *Index of Revolutionary War Pension Applications.* (Washington, D.C. 1966)

National Society, Daughters of the American Revolution. *DAR Patriot Index and Supplement.* 3rd ed. (Washington, D.C. 1966)

The Cornish and the First American Census

For genealogists, public records of all types, be they probate documents, tax lists, trial records, or real estate documents play an important role in constructing a family tree. Censuses, either taken at the local or national level are another source important to genealogists. The United States boasts one of the, if not the longest, continually recorded national census in the world. The first census, taken in 1790, was requested by President George Washington himself. The instructions required that census takers ascertain the number of inhabitants of each county or district in the thirteen states that existed at the time; to indicate the sex and color or these persons; and to enumerate the free males sixteen years of age and over. Indians were not included, but slaves were—though they appear only as numbers.

The compiling of the census had to have been a difficult task in a country that was still mostly forest only accessible by footpaths, in many cases. But most historians believe that the schedules captured the vast majority of the American population in 1790. The schedules contain over 400,000 names of heads of households, and, coupled with the numeric data included in each household, we know that the population of the United States in 1790 was at least 3,231,533.

The following is a representative sample of where the **Cornish** lived in 1790:

Benjamin Cornish, of New York, New York

Daniel Cornwell, of Spartanburg, South Carolina

Daniel, Elisha, James, Joel, Joseph Cornish, of Hartford, Connecticut

Benjamin, George, John, Josiah, Nathaniel, Samuel Cornish of Plymouth, Massachusetts

James and Jonathan Cornish, of Philadelphia, Pennsylvania

Joshua and John Cornish of Boston, Massachusetts

Eden, Samuel, and Isaac Cornwell of Litchfield, Connecticut

Ashbel, Elijah, James, William, Francis, Nathaniel, Timothy Cornwell of Middlesex, Connecticut

Melacton, Thomas, Daniel Cornwell of Albany, New York

William, Samuel, Elizabeth, Thomas, Lewis, Charles, George Cornwell, of New York, New York

Elijah Cornwell, Rowan, North Carolina

Elijah Cornwall, Wilkes, North Carolina

Nathaniel, Robert, Benjamin Cornwall, of Hartford, Connecticut

Peter and Daniel Cornwall of Middlesex, Massachusetts

Richard and Anthony Cornwall of New York, New York

Peter and William Cornell, Fayette, Pennsylvania

Rem and Giliam Cornell, Bucks, Pennsylvania

John Cornell, Lincoln, Maine

Elisha, Amos, Christopher, Daniel, and John, Stephen, and Thomas Cornell of Bristol, Massachusetts

Benjamin, Richard, and Jacob Cornell, of Frederick, Maryland

Major Cornwell, Worcester, Maryland

Joseph, Matthew, Thomas, Warrel Cornell of Albany, New York

Further Reading

William Dollarhide, *The Census Book: A Genealogists Guide to Federal Census Facts, Schedules, and Indexes* (North Salt Lake, UT, 2001)

U.S Bureau of the Census, *Heads of Families at the First Census of the United States Taken in the Year 1790*. 12 volumes. (Baltimore, 1966)

The Cornish and the Civil War

The growth of the United States occurred along with the continued spread of slavery, especially after the invention of the cotton gin opened up new land in the South to cotton production. As the United States continued to push west and take territory from Spain, Britain, and Mexico, the question of whether slavery would be legal in the new territories became a problem that no politician could ignore. This was especially true after the abolition of slavery in Britain in the 1830s gave fuel to a transatlantic abolition movement in which many Northerners took part. These Northerners were already deeply offended at the federal government's practice of returning escaped slaves to their masters in the South, and when Southerners demanded a strengthened fugitive slave act in the early 1850s, widespread civil disobedience erupted in the North. This development in turn made Southern whites more defensive and fueled their demand for federal protection of slaves in the territories. When Abraham Lincoln won the Presidential Election of 1860 on a policy of preventing any protection for slavery in the territories, six Southern states seceded from the Union. Then, after Lincoln refused to cede federal territory (Fort Sumter) in Charleston, South Carolina to the Confederacy, the Confederates opened fire and the Civil War began in April 1861.

At the start, many in the country thought the war would be over quickly. They could not have been more wrong. Over four years of fighting (most of it on Southern soil) over 620,000 soldiers died, or roughly 2% of the U.S. population. In today's terms, this would be a death toll of over 6.5 million people. The official death toll does not take into account later deaths cause by war wounds, nor does it account for the starvation, privation and disease endured by many civilians during the war that led to their deaths. Some have argued these additional fatalities mounted to as high as 150,000 people. The Civil War destroyed the South, violently ended slavery, and helped to create a bitterness among Southern whites that lasted for decades. But the war solidified the American nation, and there has not been a successful movement for secession since.

Oftentimes, the same family saw its members fight on each side of the conflict, and this was no doubt true for those named **Cornish**. According to National Park Service material **at least 400 Cornish (and** variants) fought for the Confederacy, and at least 600 Cornish (and variants) fought for the Union.

The following is a selected list of notable veterans from both the Union and the Confederacy with the surname **Cornish** or its variants:

Thomas C. Cornell (1814-1890), Major, New York Militia

Aaron Cornish, Assistant Surgeon, New York 97th Regiment

Lieutenant David Cornwall (Cornwell), Company K, 8th Illinois, author of "The Cornwell Chronicles"

Further Reading

Frank Bridgers and Meredith Colket, *Guide to Genealogical Records in the National Archives* (Washington, D.C., 1964)

C.E. Dornbusch, *Military Bibliographies of the Civil War: volumes 1 and 2, Regimental Publications and Personal Narratives* (New York, 1961-1972)

William H. Powell, *Officers of the Army and Navy (volunteer) who served in the Civil War* (Philadelphia, 1893)

Margaret Wagner, et. al., *The Library of Congress Civil War Desk Reference* (New York, 2002)

See also:

https://www.nps.gov/civilwar/soldiers-and-sailors-database.htm

African-American Cornish

The reality of slavery pervades most aspects of early American history, and the legacy of the forced enslavement of millions of Africans lives on in many ways in contemporary America. Beginning in 1619, when the first African slave was brought to the Jamestown colony, historians estimate that at least 450,000 slaves arrived either in the Thirteen Colonies or, up until about 1810, in the United States. Most of the nearly 50 million African-Americans alive today descend from these slaves.

As "chattel," or human property, there was little legal respect afforded African slaves. They could not legally marry, they had no control over their own children, and they could be sold away at a whim. Slaves also could not even meet on their own without white supervision, since white lived in constant fear of slave plots.

However, the experiences of individual slaves could vary considerably. While many slaves were essentially worked to an early grave in chains in the field, other slaves might be able to acquire a trade or even live in the master's quarters. At different times and places, it might be possible for a successful slave to buy his or her freedom, but they needed to be careful that they were not captured and sold back into slavery (slaves had no legal recourse in the courts to prevent this.)

There is also the reality that many white slavemasters fathered children with slave women. Many African-Americans are part white—and it is also the case that some light skinned African-Americans could "pass" for being white and then assimilate completely into white society, along with their offspring. The interracial background of many Southern families has only recently been openly discussed.

With emancipation in 1865, all former slaves began to use surnames, as was generally required by the federal government. In the 1870 Federal U.S. Census historians begin to see widespread use of surnames among former slaves, even as some slaves may have used surnames in private before 1865. According to historian Henry Louis Gates, Jr., most emancipated slaves took the name of their former owners—even as it seems counterintuitive that bondsmen would want to remember their owners in this way. A large number of freed African-Americans did take other names for surnames, including the names of famous people (Washington, for example) or they used the name of their occupation or hometown—and, in some cases, the former slaves chose the very appropriate name, Freeman.

Here are some African-Americans named **Cornish** and its variants:

Anita Cornwell, b. 1923, feminist author

Edward E. Cornwell, III, physician

W. Don Cornwell, b. 1948, American former CEO Granite Broadcasting

Samuel Cornish, 1795-1858, Presbyterian minister

Sandy Cornish, 1793-1869), Civic leader, Key West, Florida

Further Reading

Henry Louis Gates, *In Search of Our Roots: How 19 Extraordinary African-Americans Reclaimed Their Past* (Crown Publications, 2009)

Newbell Niles Puckett, et al, *Black Names in America: Origins and Usage* (Boston, 1975)

Julia Stewart, *1,001 African Names: first and last names from the African continent* (New York, 1996)

Cornish Pioneers

The push toward the west dated back to the colonial era, but in the nineteenth century an increasing number of Americans ventured across rugged, dangerous terrain to make their homes in places thousands of miles away from Eastern seaboard. The mid-nineteenth century was the era of the Oregon Trail, the Santa Fe trail, and other wagon train routes that made their way across the continent.

Americans of course often intruded on land that didn't belong to them, whether they were Indian tribal lands, or, before 1848, territory that belonged to another country, Mexico. The nineteenth century was a time of violent conflict over the western frontier, including the Texas Revolution of 1835, the Mexican-American War, and the various Indian Wars against tribes in the Rocky Mountain West.

Still in the period from 1820 to roughly 1900, millions of Americans moved further and further west, establishing new cities, homesteading on farms in Plains, or mining in the mountains of Far West, and as far away as

Alaska. With the admission of California in 1850, the United States extended to the Pacific; in 1867, the U.S. pushed toward the Arctic Circle after buying Alaska, and by 1893, the U.S. had annexed Hawaii in the middle of the Pacific. By 1900, increasing numbers of Americans even moved to distant shores conquered by the United States in the Spanish American War—including Panama and the Philippines.

Here are some of these notable **Cornish** pioneers, travelers, or early settlers in western frontiers:

J.L Cornish, of Anderson, Texas, before 1860

John Emory and William Cornish emigrants to Texas, before 1870

John and Matilda Cornwell, of Houston, Texas before 1850

Daniel and Sarah Cornwell in Dallas, Texas before 1860

John and Mary Cornwell of Fort Bend, Texas, before 1860

Charles Cornwell, of Yuba, California before 1850

J.N. and Henry Cornwall of Butte, California before 1850

William Cornwall of Calaveras County, California, before 1850

P.B. and Arthur Cornwall of Sacramento, California before 1850

Joseph and George Cornwall of Yam Hill, Oregon, before 1850

Alonzo Cornwell, who died in Fort Bayard, New Mexico, in 1871

Jackson and Milan Cornell, living in Tuolumne County, California before 1850

Henry Cornell of Yuba County, California before 1850

Benjamin Cornell, of El Dorado County, California before 1860

William Cornwall lived in Anchorage, Alaska in 1900

Further Reading

Native Daughters of the Golden West, California Pioneer Project (settlers before 1869):

http://www.cagenweb.com/cpl/ndgwmaster.htm

Stephenie Flora, The Oregon Territory and Its Pioneers:

http://www.oregonpioneers.com/ortrail.htm

The Original Old 300 List (Texas Settlers):

http://www.cfbca.org/Community/The_Original_Old_30_List.aspx

The Cornish and Ellis Island

The meteoric rise of the U.S. economy after the Civil War had many consequences, including an upsurge in immigration, as tens of thousands of Europeans sought new opportunities in the United States, a nation that was becoming the largest economy in the world.

The rapid industrialization, the proliferation of new technologies, and the creation of whole new industries and corporations created amazing opportunities, even as it led to the persistence of the idea of the United States as a place with as many dangers as chances for success.

There were other points of entry for the immigrants arriving to the United States after the Civil War, including Castle Garden in Manhattan, which took in arrivals from 1855 to 1890 as well as the Washington Avenue Immigration Center in Philadelphia, which processed immigrants from 1873 to 1915. The most significant—and first federally controlled—immigrant processing center, however, was at Ellis Island, in New York Harbor, which opened its doors in 1892. Most immigrants during the period 1880 to 1920 came through Ellis Island. But other immigration centers opened at the turn of the century, including the Angel Island Immigration Station in San Francisco Harbor, opened in 1910 and closed in 1940, and the East Boston Immigration Station which was open from 1920 to 1954.

It is also important to note how many immigrants in the period from 1880 to 1930 or so actually first came through Canada and were able to either legally (or in some cases illegally) cross into the U.S from her neighbor to the North. Among the ports of entry for Europeans looking to eventually make it to the U.S. were Montreal, Quebec; St. John's, Newfoundland; and Halifax, Nova Scotia.

The peak year for immigration during this period was 1907, when 1.3 million people entered the country legally. In 1917, Congress passed a law requiring immigrants over the age of 16 to pass a literacy test and, in response to increasing anxieties over immigration, Congress passed immigration restrictions, or quotas, in 1924. These quotas were not rescinded until 1965.

Here is a list of selected **Cornish** family members who arrived through Ellis Island:

Richard Cornish, arrived in 1892

L.D. Cornish, arrived in 1912

W.A. Cornwall, arrived in 1892

Lydia and Philip Cornish, 1904

Nicholas Cornish, 1905

Cyrennius Cornish of Wells, England, 1913

Amelia Cornwall, arrived in 1894

Arthur, Alicia, and George Cornwall from England in 1902

Harry Cornwall arrived in 1913

J.C. Cornwall arrived in 1914

Reginald, Grace, and Charlotte Cornwell, 1893, from England

Fred Cornell, 1893

Charles Cornwell, 1895

Sam Cornell, 1895

Silas and Jennie Cornwell, 1909

George and Albert Cornwell, 1920

John and Susan Cornell, 1907

C.F., Hugh, Ida, and Katherine Cornell, 1908

William and Joseph Cornell, 1912

Further Reading:

The Statue of Liberty-Ellis Island Foundation-Passenger List:

http://libertyellisfoundation.org/passenger

Vincent Cannato, *American Passage: the history of Ellis Island* (New York, 2009)

Loretto Denis Szucs, *Ellis Island: tracing your family tree through America's Gateway* (Provo, UT: 2000

Notable Cornish

Alonzo Cornell (1832-1904) Governor of New York

Bernard Cornwell (b.1944) British novelist

David Cornwell (b, 1945) Indiana Congressman

Ezekiel Cornell (1732-1800) Revolutionary War general and member of Continental Congress

Ezra Cornell (1807-1874) founder of Cornell University

John J. Cornwell (1867-1953) Governor of West Virginia

Marshall Cornwell (1871-1898), journalist and writer

Patricia Cornwell (b. 1956) author

Ralph Cornell (1890-1972) artist

Thomas Cornell (1814-1890) Civil War major and New York Congressman

Thomas Cornwall (1468-1537) knight and British member of parliament

William Cornish (1828-1896) Surgeon General, Madras Presidency in India

William B. Cornwell (1864-1926), businessman

William J. Cornwell (1809-1896), New York legislator

Tracing Your Cornish Roots

Most people think that constructing a family tree is difficult and tedious work, but especially with the evolution of the internet, this is, in many cases simply not true.

For anyone interested in doing their genealogy, there are several important first steps one can take:

1) Contact any of your oldest living relatives-including cousins of parents and grandparents—and ask them regarding your family. Also ask about scrap books, family albums, Bibles, antiques that might contain clues about your origins—or simply if anyone in the family has done a family tree.

2) Once you have hopefully found the names of your great-grandparents (or another, still older generation) simply type their name into google and see what turns up. Other, more focused genealogy sites include the following, where you can often find a message board for people with your last name, or other ways to

contact more experienced researchers on your family tree. Other of these sites offer you the easy option of simply plugging in the names of your ancestors and seeing what turns up:

genforum.genealogy.com, or simply genealogy.com

ancestry.com message boards (most services on ancestry.com are only accessible by subscription)

familysearch.org

findagrave.com

3) You can also see what has been posted by people doing DNA research at the following websites—most of which have surname pages where you can send out emails to people who may know something about your line, or have another way to point you towards someone who does:

familytreedna.com

23andme.com

dna.acestry.com

4) Once you have exhausted online options, you can begin accessing various kinds of records that may or may not be in existence for your ancestors. While it is true that many of these records are available through familysearch.org, or ancestry.com (for varying amounts of money), there is often no substitute for contacting the record agency itself in the town, county, or state (or province in a foreign country) where your ancestors lived. Simply google the name of the local or state Bureau of Vital Statistics, courthouse, or state library and archives for the location where you think your ancestors lived.

5) For genealogists searching in the United States, nearly every county has a historical society, as do many towns. You might be surprised what has been recorded on your family either by a local historian, or by another genealogist in many town, county, or state libraries.

6) There are also many hereditary organizations that allow researchers to see the genealogical material compiled by these organizations. Here are just a sampling of the hereditary societies that might be of use to you, especially if you are looking for early American, or colonial ancestors. Whether or not you already know that your ancestors belonged to the various groups below, it is not a bad idea to check and see if they have any information on your surname:

Aztec Club of 1847

http://www.aztecclub.com/

For family of descendants of military officers of the Mexican-American War, 1846-1848

Colonial Dames of America

http://nscda.org/

For those descended from an ancestor who came to reside in the colonies before 1776.

Dames of the Court of Honor

http://nsdch.org/public/about-us/

For descendants of commissioned officers of the early American wars between 1607 and 1865.

Daughters of the American Revolution

http://www.dar.org/

Members must descend from a man or a woman who fought for the Patriot Cause in the Revolution, or "rendered material aid thereto"

Daughters of Colonial Wars

http://nsdcw.org/

Members must be lineally descended from a military officer or political office holder before 1775.

Descendants of the Signers of the Declaration of Independence

http://www.dsdi1776.com/

Members must be lineally descended from a signer of the Declaration of Independence

Holland Society of New York

http://www.hollandsociety.com/membership.html

Members must be descended in direct male line from a Dutch settlement in the New World before 1675.

Huguenot Society of Washington, D.C.

http://www.huguenot.netnation.com/general/

Members must be descended from a French Protestant emigrant before 1787 or one who remained in France until or after the 1787 Promulgation of Toleration.

Jamestowne Society

http://www.jamestowne.org/

Members must be descended from a settler who resided in Jamestown or on Jamestowne Island before 1700.

Magna Charta Dames, National Society

http://www.magnacharta.org/

Members be lineal descendants of one or more of the Barons of England who, in or before 1215, helped secure the rights laid out in the Magna Charta

General Society of Mayflower Descendants

https://www.themayflowersociety.org/

For those descended from a passenger on the Mayflower (1620)

Order of Descendants of Colonial Governors

http://cityprideltd.com/hereditaryorderofthedescendantsofcolonialgovernors.aspx

Descendants of Governors during the colonial period.

Order of the First Families of Virginia

http://www.virginiafoundingfathers.org/

Members must descend from a qualifying ancestor mentioned in the societies roll of ancestors, who generally arrived before 1625.

Order of the Founders and Patriots of America

http://www.founderspatriots.org/

Members must descend lineally from someone who arrived before 1667, or who served as a patriot in the Revolutionary War, or who served "by making public and consistent acts manifesting adherence and loyalty to the American cause in the Revolution.

St. Nicholas Society of New York

http://www.saintnicholassociety.org/

Members must be descendants of a native or resident of the city or state of New York prior to the year 1785.

Society of the Ark and Dove

http://www.thearkandthedove.com/

For descendants of immigrants on board *The Ark* and *The Dove,* which arrived in St. Mary's, Maryland in 1634.

Sons of the American Revolution

https://www.sar.org/

For descendants of patriot soldiers, political leaders, or other who performed "overt acts or resistance to the authority of Great Britain."

Society of Colonial Wars

http://www.gscw.org/

Descendants of soldiers and politicians involved from the period before 1775.

Sons of Confederate Veterans

http://www.scv.org/

For descendants of soldiers in the Confederacy, excluding those who deserted.

Sons of Union Veterans of the Civil War

http://www.suvcw.org/

For descendants of the Union military who ancestors "have not borne arms against the Government of the United States."

United Daughters of the Confederacy

http://www.hqudc.org/

Female descendants of those who served, or from those unfit for active duty who loyally gave aid to the cause.

United States Daughters of 1812

http://www.usdaughters1812.org/

Descended from those who served in the U.S. military from 1784-1815.

General Society of the War of 1812

http://www.gsw1812.org/

Members must be male descendants of one who served during the War of 1812.

Published Cornish Genealogies

Cornell Family Association of America, *Cornell Cousins,* (Fenton, Mich, 1970-1978)

C.C. Cornell, *A Cornell Family History* (Decorah, IA, 1984)

Harrold Cornell, *Genealogy of the Cornell Family- Ezra Cornell of Wales* (Dayton, IN, 1973)

John Cornell, *Genealogy of the Cornell Family: being an account of the descendants of Thomas Cornell of Portsmouth, Rhode Island* (New York, 1902)

Thomas Cornell, *The Cornell Family of Ontario, Michigan, and Ohio* (Greentown, IN, 1990)

Edward Cornwall, *William Cornwall and his descendants* (New Haven, CT., 1901)

Emma Bennet Marshall, *Descendants of William Cornwell, of Prince William County, Virginia* (Salt Lake City, 1981)

William Claude Gould, *Cornwells of Virginia and England: A Genealogy* (Pana, Ill., 1994)

Gail Thomas Howe Cornwell, *Descendants of William Cornwell of Connecticut* (Salt Lake City, 2001)

Karen Ruth Cornwell Bowman, *The Cornwell Family History in England and the United States* (Caldwell, Idaho, 1982)

Wilnifred Cornwell Murray Milne, *The Murray Cornwell genealogies and allied families* (St. Paul, 1938)

Gale Thomas Cornwell, *Puritan Lineage from George Cornwell, 1556* (Middletown, CT, 2000)

John Cornell, *Thomas Cornell (Cornwell) 1594-1655 of Massachusetts* (Sarasota, Florida, 1975)

Jean Tibbetts, *This Land at Cornwell Farm* (Great Falls, VA, 2003)

About the Author

Ryan P. Jordan received a BA in History from UCLA (1998) and a Ph.D in History from Princeton University (2004). He is the author of several books, including *Slavery and the Meetinghouse: The Quakers and the Abolitionist Dilemma* (2007) and *Church, State, and Race: The Discourse of American Religious Liberty* (2012). He has taught at Lafayette College, the University of San Diego, and the University of California, San Diego.

www.ingramcontent.com/pod-product-compliance
Lightning Source LLC
Chambersburg PA
CBHW071224280526
45787CB00002B/796